To Lydia
Baptised in Penallt Old Church
18 September 2005
with love

To Joshua L.R.
To my sister, Alison J. R.R.

Text by Lois Rock
Illustrations copyright © 2004 Ruth Rivers
This edition copyright © 2004 Lion Publishing

The moral rights of the author and illustrator
have been asserted

Published by
Lion Publishing plc
Mayfield House, 256 Banbury Road,
Oxford OX2 7DH, England
www.lion-publishing.co.uk
ISBN 0 7459 4644 5

First edition 2004
1 3 5 7 9 10 8 6 4 2 0

Acknowledgments
The Lord's Prayer from *Common Worship: Services and Prayers
for the Church of England* (Church House Publishing, 2000) is
copyright © The English Language Liturgical Consultation, 1988.

A catalogue record for this book is available
from the British Library

Typeset in 17/24 Baskerville BT
Printed and bound in Singapore

Our Father
in Heaven

Lois Rock

Illustrated by Ruth Rivers

LION
Children's Books

When Jesus was a baby, angels sang for joy.

They said that Jesus was God's own Son.

They said he had come to bring God's blessings to the world.

When Jesus was grown up, he became a preacher.
He told stories to help people understand how
much God loves them:

more than a shepherd loves every single one
of his precious sheep;

more than a parent loves their own child.

Every day, Jesus spent time praying to God.
Sometimes he got up early and went out into
the hills where all was still and quiet.

Jesus' friends noticed that praying to God made him wiser and more joyful. They wanted to be like that too. One day, they went to Jesus and said, 'Lord, teach us to pray.'

Jesus gave them this prayer:

Our Father in heaven,

The God who made the world loves you –
more than the kindest father and the
gentlest mother.

When you look up to the great wide sky,
do not feel alone: know that God is with you.

Dear God,
Help me to know you are with me.
Help me to believe in your love.
Help me to trust in your kindness.

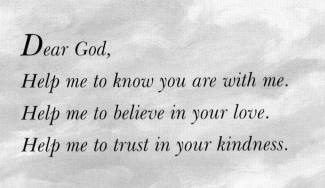

God is greater than anything in the whole wide world –

greater than the large and majestic things;

greater than the little and fragile things.

Dear God,
You are greater than anything I can
   see or imagine.
Help me to love you as you deserve.

Your kingdom come,
your will be done,
on earth as in heaven.

God is King of all the world. If everyone lived in the way that pleases God, then this world would be a better place.

*D*ear God,
Help us to love one another and to make this world more like heaven.

Give us today our daily bread.

God knows about all the things that people
need, and God has promised to take care
of us.

Dear God,
May all the people of the world
have everything they need.

God wants people to do what is good
and right.

God wants to love everyone as if the wrong
things they have done had never happened.

Dear God,
When we do wrong,
please forgive us
and help us do what
is right.

21

As we forgive those who sin against us.

God wants people to love one another as if the wrong things they have done had never happened.

*D*ear God,
Make us willing to forgive
so love and peace will grow.

Lead us not into temptation
but deliver us from evil.

Some days everything seems too hard. We
are not sure what is the right thing to do.
We feel tempted to do things that we know
are foolish and wrong.

Dear God,
Guide me in the way I go.
Lead me to a safe place.

In all his life, Jesus only did good and kind things.

Some people did not like the things he said about God. They were unhappy that so many people believed him. In the end, they had him put to death on a cross of wood.

Jesus' friends felt very sad. It seemed as if all that was bad had won. Perhaps God's love was not as strong as Jesus had said.

But three days later, Jesus' friends saw him again. He was alive. God had raised him from the dead.

Soon after, Jesus went to heaven to be with God. Before he went, he told his friends to spread the news about him to all the world: the news that God is for ever; the news that those who trust in Jesus are safe in God's love for ever and ever.

For the kingdom, the power, and the glory are yours now and for ever. Amen.

*O*ur Father in heaven,
hallowed be your name,
your kingdom come,
your will be done,
on earth as in heaven.
Give us today our daily bread.
Forgive us our sins
as we forgive those who sin against us.
Lead us not into temptation
but deliver us from evil.
For the kingdom, the power,
and the glory are yours
now and for ever.
Amen.